NEBRASKA

Past and Present

Jennifer Bringle

rosen publishing's
rosen central®

New York

To my favorite Nebraskans—Aunt Cheryl, Chris, Kim, Heidi,
Samantha, Isaiah, Hailey, and Gabriella

Published in 2011 by The Rosen Publishing Group, Inc.
29 East 21st Street, New York, NY 10010

First Edition

Library of Congress Cataloging-in-Publication Data

Bringle, Jennifer.
Nebraska: past and present / Jennifer Bringle. — 1st ed.
    p. cm. — (The United States: past and present)
Includes bibliographical references and index.
ISBN 978-1-4358-9487-7 (library binding)
ISBN 978-1-4358-9514-0 (pbk.)
ISBN 978-1-4358-9548-5 (6-pack)
1. Nebraska—Juvenile literature. I. Title.
F666.3.B67 2010
978.2—dc22

                                                                    2010002545

Manufactured in Malaysia

CPSIA Compliance Information: Batch #S10YA: For further information, contact Rosen Publishing, New York, New York, at 1-800-237-9932.

On the cover: Top left: A replica of a covered wagon near a natural rock formation in Nebraska. Top right: Fans dressed in red crowd the stands of Memorial Stadium to see the University of Nebraska Cornhuskers football team play. Bottom: A farm in the Sandhills of Nebraska.

Contents

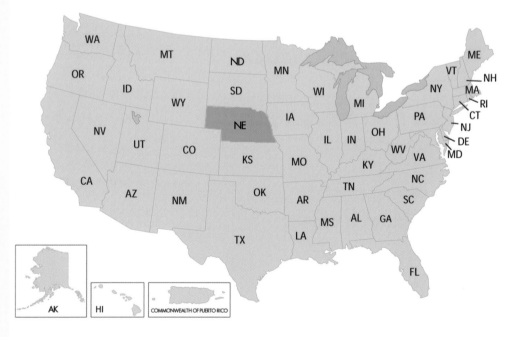

Nebraska is bordered by Colorado, Kansas, Missouri, Iowa, South Dakota, and Wyoming. The Missouri River forms the eastern border of Nebraska.

Introduction

From its days as an uncharted wilderness inhabited by Native Americans to its modern status as a thriving center of business and commerce, Nebraska has come a long way. A person standing in the middle of bustling Omaha would find it hard to believe that the state was once wild and almost empty, except for the Native American tribes that dotted the grassy landscape.

Millions of years ago, glaciers crossed the land of what would one day become Nebraska. They carved rolling hills into the otherwise flat land, setting the stage for the state's present-day landscape of grassy plains broken up by gentle hills, bluffs, and even massive sand dunes. Years later, Native Americans inhabited the land, becoming the first to make their homes in the area. As white settlers moved west in the 1800s, they brought their beliefs and traditions with them, which along with Native American customs, helped shape the state's current diverse cultural makeup.

The railroad came not long after the first homesteaders. It brought more settlers, as well as commerce, to the area. And when Nebraska was ratified as the thirty-seventh state in the Union in 1867, it was already well on its way to becoming a major player in agriculture and business.

Today, Nebraska is a leader in many areas. Major corporations such as Berkshire Hathaway, ConAgra, and Union Pacific call Nebraska home. Nebraska has come a very long way and has a bright future ahead.

Chapter 1

THE GEOGRAPHY OF NEBRASKA

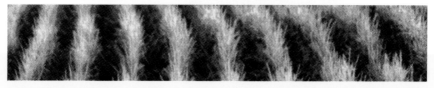

There is a popular misconception about Nebraska—that it's totally flat. While that may be true for much of the state, Nebraska does have great geographic diversity.

Two major land regions make up the state: the Dissected Till Plains and the Great Plains. Millions of years ago, during the last ice age, glaciers traveled across the eastern part of the state. Once they were gone, they left gently rolling hills that make up the Dissected Till Plains.

The Great Plains lie across most of the middle and western parts of the state. They're made up of prairie, which is a land area composed of grasslands with few or no trees. Millions of years ago, a shallow sea called the Western Interior Seaway covered the Great Plains. Once those waters receded, they left behind flat land covered with thick marine deposits. Within the Great Plains is an area called the High Plains. This area is slightly more elevated and drier, and mostly covered with short grass prairie.

The flat, rich soil of the plains makes much of Nebraska's landscape fertile. Fields of corn, wheat, and other grains and crops stretch across the state's land.

Along the plains, there are a number of unusual land formations:

Chimney Rock is located in the Panhandle region of Nebraska. It is one of the state's most recognized natural landmarks. During the westward expansion, pioneers used it as a marker along their trek.

- **The Sandhills.** Spanning almost 20,000 square miles (51,800 square kilometers), the Nebraska Sandhills are the largest sand dune formation in the Western Hemisphere.
- **Chimney Rock.** Towering more than 4,000 feet (1,219 meters), Chimney Rock is probably the most well-known geological formation in Nebraska.
- **Agate Fossil Beds National Monument.** In the 1890s, scientists discovered the fossilized bones of prehistoric creatures preserved in the rock of Carnegie and University Hills in western Nebraska. The fossil beds contained the remains of such animals as the miohippus, an ancestor of the modern horse.

Predicting Tornadoes in Nebraska

During the 1800s, homesteaders in Nebraska were at the mercy of the elements. With little warning, they hunkered down and tried to ride out storms, often losing their lives and their homes in the process.

But in 1884, U.S. Army Corps sergeant John P. Finley was placed in charge of the investigation of tornadoes and the development of forecasting methods. During an outbreak that year, he established fifteen rules for forecasting. These rules laid the groundwork for modern tornado warnings.

Forecasting made few advances until the early 1940s. During that time, the Weather Bureau formed experimental tornado warning systems with observers noting the conditions that led up to tornadoes.

In 1950, the Weather Bureau office in Norfolk and Offutt Air Force Base near Omaha participated in the Tornado Project, the first time radar was used to predict tornadoes. The data collected led to the use of radar and satellites to forecast the weather.

During the 1970s, T. Theodore Fujita introduced the F-Scale, which uses the damage caused by tornadoes to estimate their wind speed. The original scale was replaced in 2007 with the improved Enhanced Fugita Scale (EF Scale), with more accurate wind speed calculations.

Continued research and advancements in computer technology and radar have improved storm predictions. Using a combination of Doppler radar, enhanced satellite imagery, and sophisticated analysis programs, the National Weather Service has improved tornado warning lead time to fifteen minutes. Compared to the forecasting capabilities of two centuries ago, that can be the difference between life and death for Nebraskans.

- **The Missouri River.** The Missouri River runs along the eastern border of Nebraska, forming a border between the state and South Dakota, Iowa, and Missouri.
- **Courthouse and Jail Rocks.** Courthouse and Jail Rocks are two large rock formations made of Brule clay and sandstone.

Nebraska can have very harsh winters. Blizzards are a common occurrence in the state. The blizzard of 1948 left many people trapped because there were several feet of snow.

Nebraska's Climate

Like many states along the Great Plains, Nebraska often has very harsh winters, followed by hot summers.

Two major climates occur in Nebraska: the humid continental climate in the eastern half of the state and the semiarid continental steppe climate in the western part. That means the eastern part of the state is generally moister than the western part, with several more inches of precipitation per year.

During the winter, temperatures can be brutally cold. Average temperatures in January range from 11 to 39 degrees Fahrenheit (-12 to 3 degrees Celsius). The state receives an average of 30 inches (76 centimeters) of snowfall each year.

In the spring and summer, warm and moist air masses from the Gulf of Mexico stir up frequent thunderstorms. These storms can produce dangerous lightning, heavy rain, hail, and even tornadoes. Nebraska is located in the middle of a region known as Tornado Alley, due to the high number of tornadic storms that occur there. Fall is the most moderate season in Nebraska, with milder temperatures and few severe weather events.

Nebraskans have experienced some major storms that devastated the landscape. Generally, these devastating events come in one of two forms: tornadoes and blizzards.

Nebraska ranks fifth in the nation for most tornadoes. The worst of these storms occurred in Omaha in 1913. The storm killed 83 people, left 350 injured, and destroyed homes and businesses.

During the winter, blizzards can cause just as much trouble as tornadoes. In 1888, a massive blizzard blanketed the state with snow. Since the storm hit in the middle of the afternoon, many students were trapped in school because it was too dangerous to attempt walking home.

In the winter of 1948–1949, three major snowstorms in November, December, and January piled a total of 90 inches (228 cm) of snow on the state. Streets were so covered, it was nearly impossible to clear them.

Nebraska Animals

Nebraska is home to many types of wildlife, as well as farm animals. Small animals like prairie dogs and cottontail rabbits live in the heavy grasslands. Another grassland inhabitant, the black-footed ferret, is one of the most endangered animals in North America. The ferret feeds on prairie dogs, and with large portions of their habitat being plowed for farms, the species has dwindled in the past century.

Larger prairie animals include elk, pronghorn antelope, and coyotes. In 1981, the Nebraska Game and Parks Commission began a bighorn sheep introduction project in the Pine Ridge. A dozen

The sandhill crane is one of the most recognizable birds in Nebraska. Each spring, the birds migrate across the state, with thousands of birds stopping to rest by the Platte River.

bighorns were released into a 500-acre (202 hectares) enclosure. Today, the population is estimated at seventy to eighty sheep. Many birds also inhabit the prairie landscape, including bobwhite quail, wild turkeys, and prairie chickens.

Small mammals including beavers, minks, otters, raccoons, and muskrats make their homes along the rivers in Nebraska. Larger mammals like deer also live near rivers, primarily in heavy brush or wooded areas.

Endangered bird species, such as the least tern and the mountain plover, live along the state's rivers. Other waterfowl, such as whooping cranes, are also found in the state. But the sandhill crane is probably the state's most well-known bird. Each year, approximately five hundred thousand of these cranes stop to rest along the Platte River during their annual migration. From mid-February to mid-April, the cranes can be seen and heard for 30 miles (48 km) along the river.

While many wild animals call Nebraska home, millions of farm animals also populate the state. The most common of these animals are cattle, which are raised for Nebraska's large beef production and dairy industries. In fact, cows outnumber people in the state, almost four to one. Many different breeds of cattle live on Nebraska farms, including Black Angus, Hereford, longhorn, and Scottish highland. Nebraska is also a big pork-producing state, so it's home to thousands of pigs and hogs, too.

Nebraska Plants

Because of Nebraska's relatively dry climate, the state's vegetation is primarily grassland. The western prairie is mostly covered with tall bluestem grass, which also covers much of the Sandhills area. The panhandle portion of the state is covered with short, sparse grama and buffalo grass. Sagebrush can also be found in this region. A mix of sand sage and short grasses covers the sandy plains of the southwest.

Only about 2 percent of the state is forestland. Trees primarily grow in river valleys and on higher sandstone formations in the northwestern region. In the eastern portion of the state, oak, hickory, and elm trees are most common. Farther west, the river valleys are lined with cottonwood, willow, and elm trees. Ponderosa pines grow on some elevated areas of the Great Plains and in the Nebraska

Nebraska is one of the largest corn-producing states in the nation. The crop is the main agricultural plant grown in the state. Nebraska's state nickname, the Cornhusker State, reflects its corn production.

National Forest. The forest is the largest hand-planted forest in the country, with 90,000 acres (36,422 ha) of woodland.

In addition to wild plants, the state is covered with acres of crops. The most prevalent of these is corn. Corn is so popular that Nebraska's state nickname is the Cornhusker State. Millions of acres of corn are planted each year. The corn is used for food production, as well as for livestock feed and other purposes, such as ethanol gas.

Soybeans are an important crop in Nebraska. Covering millions of acres, soybean plants bring millions of dollars into the state's economy each year. Wheat is another major farm crop in the state.

Chapter 2

THE HISTORY OF NEBRASKA

While many people think of the pioneers as the first residents of Nebraska, the Native Americans made their home there long before the homesteaders headed west. Centuries before Nebraska became a state, many of the great nations of the central plains ruled the land.

The Omaha, Otoe-Missouria, Arapaho, Cheyenne, Pawnee, Lakota, and Ponca were just a few of the major tribes that inhabited prestate Nebraska. Many of their traditions and cultural aspects, including their names, have endured to present-day Nebraska.

During the 1800s, as pioneers began moving westward, the new settlers and the U.S. military began to clash with the Native Americans. As the natives began to fight back against those invading their land, several leaders began to emerge from the tribes. Red Cloud rose to prominence as a warrior of the Oglala Lakota. He opposed westward expansion, first by fighting against the settlers and the military. Eventually, he took the role of negotiator, trying to work with the U.S. government to help protect and preserve his people's way of life.

During the westward expansion, many tribes were forced by the government to give up their land. Several treaties took land from Nebraska tribes. During this time, many Native Americans were moved to reservations, either within the territory or in neighboring Oklahoma. Today, some of those reservations still remain, a reminder of past injustices toward Native Americans.

The Westward Expansion

After the Louisiana Purchase in 1803, President Thomas Jefferson sent explorers west to find a waterway leading to the Pacific Ocean. Meriwether Lewis and William Clark led the expedition. The explorers visited the territory that would eventually become Nebraska, learning about the Missouri River and discovering previously unknown animals, such as the prairie dog.

Not long after the Lewis and Clark expedition, pioneers began packing wagons and traveling west to settle.

As white settlers moved into the Nebraska Territory, famous Native American chiefs, such as Red Cloud and American Horse, led their tribes against the American military.

Following trails like the Oregon Trail and the Mormon Trail, settlers crossed Nebraska and made their homes on the state's prairie. During this time, the government built forts to help protect settlers. In Nebraska, forts including Atkinson, Omaha, Crook, Kearny, and Plum Creek Station helped protect settlers from Native American attacks.

In 1854, the federal government passed the Kansas-Nebraska Act, which officially designated these two territories for settlement. With

The Railroad in Nebraska

During the nineteenth and much of the twentieth centuries, the railroad was a major economic force in Nebraska. It helped settle the state during the westward expansion, and it helped farmers grow their business by transporting their crops to all corners of the nation. Many different railroads had a stake in Nebraska, with nearly a dozen receiving land grants from the government.

For many years, trains were the fastest and most efficient means of transportation. So passenger trains, as well as freight trains, crossed Nebraska for many years. These trains brought people from other states to towns along the railroad, bringing new settlers and visitors who spent money in those towns.

But during the early part of the twentieth century, things began to change. Automobiles were invented, and paved roads began popping up across the country. With the establishment of the Interstate Highway System during the 1950s, more people traveled in cars than trains. And trucks began carrying more freight than trains. The invention of the airplane also affected railroads' popularity. It took even more travelers and freight traffic from railroads.

Today, the railroad is still the primary means of transporting products such as coal and grain. But it no longer has the monopoly on transportation that it had during the homestead era. And though the railroad isn't the major entity in Nebraska that it once was, Union Pacific's Bailey Yard in North Platte is still the largest classification yard in the world. It is a crossroads for rail lines in North America, making Nebraska the center for rail traffic.

this act, the Nebraska Territory stretched far beyond present-day state borders. During this time, many of the Native American tribes were forced to give up their land to settlers. This caused a great conflict between Native Americans and white settlers.

In 1862, the government passed the Homestead Act. This legislation gave 160 acres (65 ha) of public land to any head of household who lived on the land for five years. This encouraged many to move to the Nebraska Territory to establish farms.

During this time, many immigrants from foreign countries settled in Nebraska. The promise of "free" land drew many immigrants, who were peasants in their former countries and unable to afford land. Of these settlers, many were Czechs. But Swedish, German, Irish, and Polish settlers also inhabited the land.

As the territory became populated, the U.S. government moved to make it an official state. In 1867, Nebraska became the thirty-seventh state in the Union.

The Railroad

At the same time that settlers were getting land through the Homestead Act, the federal government was granting large tracts of land throughout the plains to the railroad. The government hoped there would be tracks where no one lived, which would help further the settlement of these areas. It also hoped the railroad would link the East Coast to the West Coast, opening a trade line between the East Coast and Asian countries.

The Union Pacific Railroad, which is still headquartered in Omaha, and the Burlington Railroad were the two major railroads going through Nebraska. The growth of the railroad changed westward expansion by making it much easier for settlers to move west. Instead

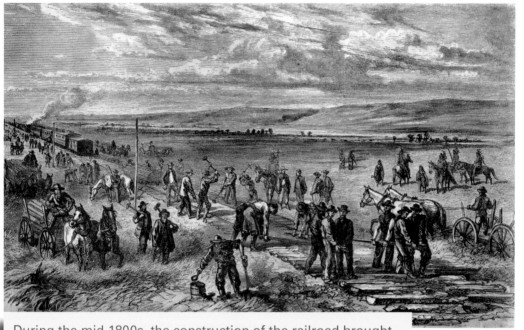

During the mid-1800s, the construction of the railroad brought many settlers to Nebraska. As the Union Pacific line laid tracks across the state, more businesses and towns popped up.

of braving the dangers of covered wagon travel, they could travel by train to settle the land around the railroad. Eventually, the railroad began selling some of its land to settlers who wanted to be closer to the railroad. This made sense for farmers because they wanted to be close to trains that would transport crops to other parts of the country.

The railroad grew as farming grew in Nebraska. Agriculture and rail business depended on each other. Soon, the railroad began to employ more and more Nebraskans. As it prospered, the railroad became a prominent part of Nebraska's politics, economy, and culture.

Modern Nebraska

During the twentieth century, Nebraska played a role in many major events. During World War II, the state hosted nearly twelve thousand prisoners of war at several camps. Scottsbluff, Fort Robinson, and the village of Atlanta were the main base camps, with smaller camps throughout

During World War II, camps housing prisoners held by the American military were built in Nebraska. The presence of these enemy soldiers brought the reality of war home to Nebraskans.

the state. Before the war even began, Nebraska was chosen as the headquarters for several weaponry plants. The Martin Bomber Plant opened in 1941 and began building bomber planes. Ammunition plants were opened in several cities. Nebraska was attractive for these kinds of operations because it was far from the coast and thus far from foreign invaders.

In the 1970s, Nebraska farmers were hit hard by a bad economy and extreme droughts. As the 1980s approached, there was a major decline in the state's agriculture industry, which caused many farmers to go into financial ruin. Many farms were lost to foreclosure. Families were forced to leave their homes and their source of income. The 1970s and 1980s were difficult decades for Nebraska farmers. And as the 1990s and the new century came, many people abandoned farming for other industries. Today, farming is no longer the dominant industry in Nebraska.

Chapter 3

THE GOVERNMENT OF NEBRASKA

Nebraska's government operates according to the state's constitution, which was adopted in 1875. The government is divided into three branches: the executive branch, the legislative branch, and the judicial branch.

The Executive Branch

The governor heads Nebraska's executive branch. He or she is elected to a four-year term and is limited to serving a maximum of two consecutive terms. The governor's second in command is the lieutenant governor. The lieutenant governor is also elected to a four-year term, which have no limit. Should the governor die, resign, or be removed from office, the lieutenant governor takes over the position.

Other elected officers of the executive branch include the attorney general, the secretary of state, the state treasurer, and the state auditor. These officials also serve four-year terms.

The governor's duties include signing or vetoing bills passed by the legislature, acting as chief budget officer for the state, appointing certain officers to fill vacancies in state offices, and enforcing criminal laws. The lieutenant governor presides over the legislature,

The governor leads Nebraska's executive branch of government. The governor signs or vetoes bills passed by the legislature. He or she works in the city of Lincoln and lives in the governor's mansion, which is also located there.

performs duties assigned by the governor, and fills in for or replaces the governor if he or she cannot serve.

The Legislative Branch

Nebraska is the only state in the nation with a unicameral legislature. This means the legislature has only one house, not two like most states. Senator George Norris encouraged the idea of the unicameral legislature. Norris and his supporters argued that a two-house legislature was inefficient and undemocratic, as it featured committees that held secret elections. In 1934, the unicameral legislature was established by a state initiative.

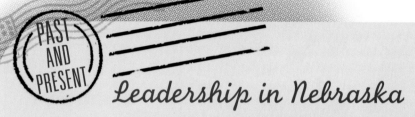

Leadership in Nebraska

Since people first settled what is now Nebraska, there have been great leaders who helped protect and unify the state's people. In the early days, before Nebraska was even a state, great chiefs led the Native American nations. Leaders such as Red Cloud, who led the Oglala, and Standing Bear, who led the Ponca, were in their time quite similar to a present-day governor. They promoted the causes of their people and worked to preserve their rights and maintain order. Many times, they tried to work along with the U.S. government to achieve these goals, just as a governor does when representing his or her state on a national level. But unlike governors, these Native American leaders strongly clashed with the government. They led their warriors in battle against settlers and the military.

As white settlers populated Nebraska and the state was officially established, leadership changed. Instead of mighty chieftains, governors and legislators led the state's people. Francis Burt became Nebraska's first governor when it was still a territory. A South Carolina legislator, Burt was sent to the Nebraska Territory to serve as its governor but died in Bellevue two days after arriving. Thomas B. Cuming replaced him.

In the years since those territory governors, more than forty governors have led Nebraska. Modern governors have different concerns and duties. The governor must make sure the state's laws are properly executed, act as the state's chief budget officer, and sign bills into law, among other duties. Since the days of warrior chiefs, leadership in Nebraska has come a long way and gotten much more complicated.

The members of the house are called senators, and they represent different districts from all over the state. Nebraska's state legislature is nonpartisan, which means senators are elected with no party affiliation next to their name on the ballot. The speaker and committee chairs are chosen at large, so members of any party can be chosen for these positions. Nebraska is the only state in the Union with a nonpartisan legislature. Nebraska's legislature can override the governor's veto with a three-fifths majority. In many other states, a two-thirds majority is required.

The State Capitol building in Lincoln houses Nebraska's unicameral legislature, which means the legislature only has one house.

The legislature meets in the Nebraska State Capitol building in Lincoln. Built between 1922 and 1932, the domed capitol building is known for the Golden Sower statue on its roof. The bronze statue, of a woman planting seeds, represents the state's agricultural heritage.

The Judicial Branch

Nebraska's judicial system is unified, meaning the state supreme court has authority over all Nebraska courts. The lowest courts are county courts. Then there are twelve district courts. Next is the court of appeals, which hears appeals from district courts, juvenile courts, and worker's compensation courts. The supreme court is the highest

Nebraska's Supreme Court serves as the highest court in the state. It is made up of a chief justice and six associate justices.

court and the final word on appeals.

The supreme court consists of a chief justice and six associate justices. The governor appoints the chief justice. The other justices are chosen by a judicial nominating committee and represent the state's six districts.

The supreme court hears appeals and provides administrative leadership for the rest of the judicial system. It's also responsible for regulation of the practice of law in Nebraska.

The court of appeals consists of six judges appointed by the governor. It is divided into two panels of three judges each in order to process appeals quickly. District courts have the same jurisdiction as county courts, but they primarily hear felony cases, criminal cases, equity cases, and civil cases involving more than $51,000.

Nebraska judges are selected through the merit system. When a judge leaves the post for whatever reason, a judicial nominating commission chooses the vacant position. The commission, made up of lawyers selected by the Nebraska State Bar, holds a public hearing to interview candidates. The commission then submits two names to the governor and the governor chooses the new judge.

Chapter 4

The Economy of NEBRASKA

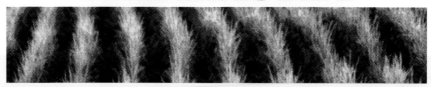

Since the state of Nebraska was first settled, its economy has been based on agriculture, specifically raising livestock and growing corn and wheat. During the 1930s, the Great Depression and a long drought threatened the state's agricultural industry and its economy in general. But in the years since, a better economy and innovations in farm irrigation have rebuilt the state's agricultural base. Today, more than 90 percent of the state's land is devoted to farms and ranches.

Nebraska is a national leader in crop production. In recent years, Nebraska's farmers have led the nation in the production of great northern beans and popcorn. Nebraska is also a major producer of pinto beans, corn, alfalfa hay, and grain sorghum. More than 8 million acres (3 million ha) of the state's land are devoted to corn.

The state also produces many products related to agriculture. Irrigation systems and farm equipment are manufactured in the state. One in three jobs in Nebraska relate to the agriculture industry.

Another major part of Nebraska's economy is the railroad. Since the railroad helped settle the state in the 1800s, it has been a huge employer and facilitator of business in the state. Many farmers depend on the railroad to transport their crops around the country. The railroad also employs a large number of Nebraskans. Union

Much of Nebraska's economy is based on agriculture. The state grows and produces crops that are sold all over the world. These crops also go into food products that are produced by companies such as Omaha's ConAgra.

Pacific is the third largest private employer in the state, with more than seven thousand employees.

Although Nebraska's economy is still agricultural, more of the state's income has come from other industries in recent years. Manufacturing, which employs hundreds of thousands of workers, is one of the state's major nonfarming industries. Food processing is the leading type of manufacturing, followed by machinery and fabricated metal product manufacturing.

Nebraska is also home to several major national companies that significantly contribute to the state's economy. Berkshire Hathaway, a holding and investment firm run by billionaire Warren Buffett, is based in Omaha. It is regularly one of the nation's Fortune 500 companies. (The Fortune 500 is an annual list by *Fortune* magazine of the largest industrial and service corporations in the United States, based on revenue.) Also regularly making that list is ConAgra, also based in Omaha. ConAgra is a food processing and marketing

Nebraska Industry

Through the years, Nebraska's industry has changed significantly. During the early days of the state, its economy was almost entirely based on agriculture. Farming was the chief business in Nebraska, and the growing and selling of crops and livestock funded the young state. At the time, there really weren't large cities there, so most of the state's populated areas were small towns surrounded by acres of farms.

During the 1930s, things began to change. As the Great Depression began to take hold of the nation, economic troubles began in Nebraska, too. As the market dropped, so did the prices for crops. Farmers made less money and were struggling just as much as those in other industries across the nation. To make matters worse, a terrible drought plagued the region, turning the heartland into a dust-bowl. Crops withered without water, and farmers had nothing to sell or feed their families and livestock.

In the decades since those rough times, agriculture has rebounded in Nebraska. But alongside it, new industries have emerged and taken over a large chunk of the state's economy. With the success of Warren Buffett and his firm, Berkshire Hathaway, Nebraska has become a major player in the financial industry. Financial companies such as TD Ameritrade and Nelnet, and insurance leaders such as Mutual of Omaha and Woodmen of the World, have all established major operations in Nebraska.

Other industries, such as manufacturing, have also established a large presence in Nebraska. With major corporations such as food producer ConAgra and engineering and construction firm Peter Kiewit Sons, Nebraska's manufacturing industry is becoming a major force in the state's economy.

With so much economic diversity, Nebraska stands ready to weather another economic downturn. And as before, it'll come out on top.

ConAgra, which is based in Omaha, produces many of America's best-known food products. Major brands such as Chef Boyardee, Orville Redenbacher, and Healthy Choice are all produced by ConAgra.

company that produces many major grocery store brands, including Chef Boyardee, Orville Redenbacher, and Healthy Choice.

Several other Fortune 500 companies have major operations in Nebraska. They include TD Ameritrade, a financial and securities firm with offices in Omaha, and Cabela's, a hunting/outdoor retailer with its main office in Sydney.

Chapter 5

PEOPLE FROM NEBRASKA:
PAST AND PRESENT

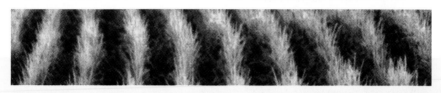

Many outstanding people have lived in Nebraska. Some of these people have achieved such great success that they are world famous for their contributions.

Historical Figures

Crazy Horse (1849–1877) One of the most famous Native American chiefs, Crazy Horse lived in Nebraska before it became a state. A member of the Lakota tribe, he fought alongside Oglala chief Red Cloud against settlers and the army. When the U.S. War Department ordered all Lakota bands onto reservations in 1876, Crazy Horse led the resistance. Along with members of other tribes, including Sitting Bull, he fought against General George Armstrong Custer at Little Bighorn. Crazy Horse encouraged other Native Americans to stand strong on keeping their traditions alive and resist the changes being forced upon them by white settlers. He was forced to surrender to the U.S. military in 1877. Shortly thereafter, a soldier killed him.

Malcolm X (1925–1965) One of the most recognizable names of the civil rights movement, Malcolm X was born

Crazy Horse was one of the most famous Native American chiefs. A member of the Lakota tribe, Crazy Horse fought alongside Oglala chief Red Cloud against the U.S. military invasion.

Malcolm Little in Omaha. As a baby, his family moved to Michigan, where he grew up. In his youth, Malcolm X got into trouble for petty crimes and ultimately served time in prison. While in prison, he converted to Islam and joined the primarily black Nation of Islam. Once released, he became active in the black nationalist and civil rights movements. A charismatic speaker, Malcolm X became a leader for African American freedom fighters in the United States. In 1965, he was assassinated as he gave a speech in Harlem.

Red Cloud (1822–1909) Red Cloud was one of the most important Native American leaders in the nineteenth century. Born near what is now North Platte, Red Cloud was a member of the Oglala band. Much of his early life was spent at war with neighboring tribes. During the middle part of the century, however, his efforts shifted to fighting the U.S. military and western settlers. In 1866, he staged the most successful war against the United States ever fought by

Native Americans. The town of Red Cloud in Nebraska is named for him.

Nebraskans in the Arts

Fred Astaire (1899–1987) Arguably one of the best dancers of the golden age of Hollywood, Fred Astaire was born in Omaha. He began dancing at the age of four. His professional career began when he was cast as a dancer in musicals. Eventually, he became a major star along with his dancing partner Ginger Rogers. Astaire starred in more than thirty films. He received an honorary Oscar for his film achievements in 1950.

Marlon Brando, one of the most famous Hollywood actors of the last century, was born in Omaha. Brando is best known for playing Don Corleone in *The Godfather*.

Marlon Brando (1924–2004) With his mother actively involved in the Omaha Community Playhouse, it's no wonder Omaha native Marlon Brando went on to become an actor. After a childhood spent in Nebraska and Illinois, Brando moved to New York City to study acting. He then moved to Hollywood to act in films. During his youth, he starred in such films as *A Streetcar Named Desire* and *On the Waterfront*, for which he won an Oscar. Brando won another Oscar for his portrayal of mafia boss Don Corleone in *The Godfather* in 1972.

Johnny Carson (1925–2005) The original "king of late night," Johnny Carson grew up in Nebraska and graduated from the University of Nebraska. After graduation, he worked for a radio station in Omaha before leaving Nebraska to work at a television station in Los Angeles. In 1962, Carson was chosen to take over as host of *The Tonight Show*. He hosted the show for forty years, retiring in 1992. During his time as a host, Carson won several Emmys and other honors.

Willa Cather (1873–1947) Writing about the lives of pioneers on the frontier, Willa Cather became one of America's most respected novelists. She was born in Virginia, but as a child, her family relocated to the village of Red Cloud. After graduating from the University of Nebraska, she worked at several publications in Pennsylvania and New York. In 1912, Cather began writing novels. She wrote about the people and places that she knew in Nebraska in books such as *O Pioneers!*, *My Antonia*, and *One of Ours*, which won a Pulitzer Prize.

Henry Fonda (1905–1982) Born in Grand Island, Henry Fonda went on to become one of Hollywood's greatest actors. Fonda spent his childhood and teen years in Omaha, where he was introduced to theater by Marlon Brando's mother, Dorothy, at the Omaha Community Playhouse.

Writer Willa Cather grew up in Red Cloud, Nebraska. She wrote many of her books there, basing some of her characters on people she knew. *O Pioneers!* and *My Antonia* are both set in Nebraska.

Fonda appeared in films such as *Young Mr. Lincoln* and *The Grapes of Wrath*. Fonda had several children, including the actors Peter and Jane Fonda. He starred with his daughter Jane in his final film, *On Golden Pond*, in 1981. He won the Oscar for Best Actor for the film.

Marg Helgenberger (1958–) Born in Fremont, Marg Helgenberger attended Kearney State College before transferring to Northwestern University. Although she won an Emmy for her role on the 1980s television show *China Beach*, Helgenberger is probably best known today for acting in the popular crime drama *CSI*.

Larry the Cable Guy (1963–) Born Dan Whitney in Pawnee City, Larry the Cable Guy rose to fame with his down-home humor. The comedian grew up on a farm, but his family moved to Florida in 1979. During the early days of his career, he performed under his real name, doing routine stand-up comedy. But after an appearance on a radio show in character as a southern-accented "hick," Whitney's stage persona was born.

Conor Oberst (1980–) Singer-songwriter Conor Oberst was born in Omaha. The lead singer of folk rock band Bright Eyes, Oberst started playing music at the age of fourteen. As a teen, Oberst and his older brothers set up a record label that would eventually become Saddle Creek Records, the label Oberst operates in Omaha.

Hilary Swank (1974–) Born in Lincoln, Hilary Swank began acting as a teenager, but she didn't achieve stardom until her Oscar-winning role in 1999's *Boys Don't Cry*. She starred in many more films, winning another Oscar in 2005 for *Million Dollar Baby*.

Nebraskans in Business

Warren Buffett (1930–) Named the second wealthiest man in the United States, Omaha native Warren Buffett is one of the most successful businessmen in history. He demonstrated skill in financial and business matters from an early age. His father, who was a stockbroker and U.S. congressman, encouraged his interest.

Nebraska native Warren Buffett is the second wealthiest man in the United States. A University of Nebraska graduate, Buffett and his company, Berkshire Hathaway, are based in Omaha.

During his childhood, Buffett had a number of businesses, including a small pinball machine business. He graduated from the University of Nebraska, and in 1956, he formed the firm Buffett Partnership in Omaha. With his firm, he made investments and bought undervalued companies, amassing a great fortune. Buffet was estimated by *Forbes* in 2008 to be worth $62 billion.

Joyce C. Hall (1891–1982) While other kids were earning money on paper routes, Joyce C. Hall was pooling his money

Nebraska's Music

Nebraska music has made significant changes through the years. In the state's early days, traditional Native American songs were the sound of Nebraska. Characterized by strong drumbeats and chanting, these songs were used as entertainment, as well as a means of communication among the tribes.

As the westward expansion brought settlers to Nebraska, cowboy or western music began to grow popular throughout the land. A predecessor of what is now known as country music, these songs were folk-based and often about the lives of cowboys, farmers, and other hardworking settlers. These songs were often shared at town get-togethers and around cowboy campfires on the range.

During the modern era, Nebraska's music and musicians have become quite varied. In the 1920s–1960s, north Omaha became a vibrant music and entertainment district for African American music. The neighborhood's jazz and R&B scene thrived during this time, especially at the legendary Dreamland Ballroom. This venue hosted both local acts, as well as national performers such as Nat King Cole and Duke Ellington.

Perhaps some of the most recognized Nebraska musicians today are the alt-rock and folk-rock bands in Omaha, which are known for playing the Omaha sound. Groups such as Bright Eyes, The Faint, and Cursive are noted for this sound, and have all made a name for themselves on the national music scene. Saddle Creek Records, run by Bright Eyes lead singer Conor Oberst, has released albums by many of the "Omaha sound" bands. Oberst and his record label partners also opened their own music venue, Slowdown, in downtown Omaha. The venue is unique because it combines a live music venue with shops, restaurants, and apartments, making it a hub for artists and musicians.

The success of these groups serves as inspiration for future Nebraska musicians to continue the state's musical legacy.

with his brothers to start a business. The Norfolk native founded Hallmark Cards.

In the beginning, it was a postcard business run by teenagers. Things didn't go well at first, but Hall persevered. He hit the road at the age of eighteen with shoeboxes full of his cards. He traveled to Kansas City, selling his cards to drugstores, bookshops, and gift shops. Eventually, the business took off, and Hall and his brothers opened a store in Kansas City.

Edwin Perkins (1889–1961) Though his name might not sound familiar, just about every kid in America is familiar with the invention of Hastings native Edwin Perkins. In 1927, Perkins invented Kool-Aid. He had experimented with chemistry since his childhood, creating a number of products like deodorant and foot powder. But Perkins didn't really hit it big until creating the powdered beverage loved by kids to this day.

Evan Williams (1972–) Taking advantage of the popularity of social networking, Evan Williams has built a successful business with his Internet companies Pyra Labs, which created the blogging site Blogger, and Twitter. Williams was born in Clarks. He attended the University of Nebraska and after leaving school, had several technology jobs. In 2007, Williams helped create Twitter, a social networking site. By 2009, Twitter took off and became one of the most popular social networking sites in the world.

Timeline

1803	The Louisiana Purchase gives the land that will become Nebraska to the United States.
1804	Lewis and Clark explore the land that will become Nebraska.
1830	The Oregon Trail brings pioneers westward through Nebraska.
1848	Fort Kearny is established along the Oregon Trail.
1854	The Kansas-Nebraska Act establishes the Nebraska Territory.
1862	The Homestead Act gives land in the Nebraska Territory to settlers; the Union Pacific Railroad is chartered.
1867	Nebraska becomes a state; the first railroad across the state is completed.
1869	The University of Nebraska, Lincoln, is established.
1872	J. Sterling Morton founds Arbor Day in Nebraska City.
1919	ConAgra is founded as Nebraska Consolidated Mills.
1924	Native Americans are granted citizenship.
1927	Edwin Perkins invents Kool-Aid in Hastings.
1929	The stock market crashes, bringing the Great Depression to Nebraska.
1943	World War II prisoner-of-war camps are set up in Nebraska.
1962	Warren Buffett begins the takeover of Berkshire Hathaway.
1977	The farm crisis hits Nebraska farmers, causing massive profit losses.
1993	Conor Oberst and his brother found Omaha record label Saddle Creek Records.
2008	The J. Robert Kerrey Pedestrian Bridge opens in Omaha, becoming the longest pedestrian bridge to link two states, Nebraska and Iowa.

State motto:	"Equality Before the Law"
State capital:	Lincoln
State tree:	Western cottonwood
State bird:	Western meadowlark
State flower:	Goldenrod
Statehood date and number:	March 1, 1867; thirty-seventh state
State nickname:	The Cornhusker State
Total area and U.S. rank:	77,358 square miles (200,356 sq km); sixteenth largest state
Population:	1,783,000
Highest elevation:	Panorama Point, near the western border, at 5,426 feet (1,654 m)
Lowest elevation:	In the southeast, at 840 feet (256 m)

State flag

State seal

Major rivers:	Missouri River, Platte River, Niobrara River
Major lakes:	Lake McConaughy, Lewis and Clark Lake
Highest recorded temperature:	118°F (48°C), at Minden, July 24, 1936
Lowest recorded temperature:	-47°F (-8°C), at Camp Clarke, February 12, 1899
Origin of state name:	From an Otoe Indian word that means "flat water"
Chief agricultural products:	Corn, dry edible beans, alfalfa hay, grain sorghum
Major industries:	Agriculture, manufacturing, finance

Western meadowlark

Goldenrod

GLOSSARY

alfalfa A flowering plant in the pea family grown for livestock feed.

appeal A legal procedure where a court decision by a lower court is brought before a higher court for consideration.

homestead An area measuring around 160 acres (65 ha) that includes a farm and a house for farmers.

humid continental climate Moister climate found in the eastern part of Nebraska; signifies more precipitation.

jurisdiction The power, right, or authority to apply the law.

Native American A person whose ancestors inhabited the United States before it was settled by Europeans; also sometimes referred to as "Indian" or "American Indian."

nonpartisan Not having or declaring a political party affiliation.

pioneer A person who is one of the first to settle a new territory.

prairie Flat land area composed of grasslands with few or no trees.

prairie dog A burrowing rodent found in grasslands, similar to a squirrel.

reservation Land specified by the federal government for Native Americans after their land was taken for settlers.

semiarid continental steppe climate The drier climate found in the western part of Nebraska.

sorghum A grass species used for food, livestock feed, and other products.

territory A geographic area belonging to, or under the authority of, a government.

unicameral Describing a legislature consisting of one legislative house, rather than a house of representatives and a senate.

Nebraska Department of Economic Development

301 Centennial Mall South

Lincoln, NE 68509

(800) 426-6505

Web site: http://www.neded.org

The Nebraska Department of Economic Development oversees the state's economic development and helps promote the state.

Nebraska Game and Parks Commission

2200 N. 33rd Street

Lincoln, NE 68503

(402) 471-0641

Web site: http://www.ngpc.state.ne.us

The Nebraska Game and Parks Commission manages parks and wildlife in the state in the long-term interests of the people and resources of Nebraska.

Nebraska Library Commission

1200 N Street, Suite 120

Lincoln, NE 68508

(402) 471-2045

Web site: http://www.nlc.state.ne.us

The Nebraska Library Commission oversees the state's libraries and serves as a source of information for research.

Nebraska State Historical Society

1500 R Street

Lincoln, NE 68501

(402) 471-3270

Web site: http://www.nebraskahistory.org

The Nebraska State Historical Society collects and preserves the state's historical records and stories.

Visit Nebraska—Nebraska Travel & Tourism

301 Centennial Mall South

Lincoln, NE 68509

(888) 444-1867

Web site: http://www.visitnebraska.gov

Nebraska Travel & Tourism promotes the state and all it has to offer to tourists, as well as citizens.

Willa Cather Foundation

413 N. Webster

Red Cloud, NE 68970

(866) 731-7304

Web site: http://www.willacather.org

The Willa Cather Foundation works to preserve the memory of Nebraska author Willa Cather. It also maintains the Willa Cather Memorial Prairie in Red Cloud.

Web Sites

Due to the changing nature of Internet links, Rosen Publishing has developed an online list of Web sites related to the subject of this book. This site is updated regularly. Please use this link to access the list:

http://www.rosenlinks.com/uspp/nepp

FOR FURTHER READING

Cather, Willa. *O Pioneers!* New York, NY: Random House, 1989.

Figley, Marty Rhodes. *The Schoolchildren's Blizzard* (On My Own History). Minneapolis, MN: Carolrhoda Books, 2004.

Hanel, Rachel. *Nebraska* (This Land Called America). Mankato, MN: Creative Education, 2009.

Luebke, Frederick C. *Nebraska: An Illustrated History*. Lincoln, NE: University of Nebraska Press, 2005.

McMurtry, Larry. *Crazy Horse*. New York, NY: Penguin, 2005.

Meltzer, Milton. *Willa Cather: A Biography*. Minneapolis, MN: Twenty-First Century Books, 2007.

Monroe, Judy. *Chief Red Cloud: 1822–1909*. Mankato, MN: Blue Earth Books, 2003.

Ollhoff, Jim. *Nebraska* (The United States). Edina, MN: Checkerboard Press, 2009.

Schroeder, Alice. *The Snowball: Warren Buffett and the Business of Life*. New York, NY: Bantam, 2009.

Stanley, George E. *Crazy Horse: Young War Chief*. Fullerton, CA: Aladdin Books, 2005.

Weatherly, Myra S. *Nebraska* (From Sea to Shining Sea). Danbury, CT: Children's Press, 2009.

Zollman, Pam. *Nebraska* (Rookie Read-About Geography). Danbury, CT: Children's Press, 2007.

BIBLIOGRAPHY

Bonanno, Alessandro, ed. *From Columbus to ConAgra: The Globalization of Agriculture and Food*. Lawrence, KS: University Press of Kansas, 1994.

Boyne, Alan. *The Complete Roadside Guide to Nebraska*. Lincoln, NE: Bison Books, 2007.

Federal Writers Project. *Nebraska: A Guide to the Cornhusker State*. Lincoln, NE: University of Nebraska Press, 2006.

Hallmark Corporation. "Founder Joyce C. Hall." Retrieved October 5, 2009 (http://corporate.hallmark.com/history/founder-jc-hall).

Hetzel, Kate, ed. *The Nebraska Blue Book*. Lincoln, NE: Clerk of the Legislature's Office, 2009.

High Plains Regional Climate Center. "Tornado Statistics." Retrieved August 23, 2009 (http://www.hprcc.unl.edu/nebraska/NEBTORNADOFACTS.html).

Kaercher, Dan. *Best of the Midwest: Rediscovering America's Heartland*. Guilford, CT: Globe Pequot Press, 2005.

McNally, Hannah. *Nebraska: A Guide to Unique Places* (Off the Beaten Path). Guilford, CT: Globe Pequot Press, 2007.

National Oceanic and Atmospheric Administration. "History of Tornado Forecasting." Retrieved August 23, 2009 (http://celebrating200years.noaa.gov/magazine/tornado_forecasting/welcome.html).

National Oceanic and Atmospheric Administration. "Omaha Easter Tornado." Retrieved August 23, 2009 (http://www.crh.noaa.gov/oax/archive/1913_Omaha_Tor/omaha tornado.php).

Nebraska Division of Travel and Tourism. *The Nebraska Travel Guide*. 2009, pp. 20–21.

Nebraska Emergency Management Agency. "Tornado Facts and Information." Retrieved August 23, 2009 (http://www.nema.ne.gov/index_html?page=content/disaster_recovery/tornadofacts.html).

Nebraska Judicial Branch. "Overview of the Nebraska Court System." Retrieved August 22, 2009 (http://supremecourt.ne.gov/press/guide.shtml).

Nebraska Legislature. "History of Nebraska Unicameral." Retrieved August 22, 2009 (http://nebraskalegislature.gov/about/history_unicameral.php).

Nebraska State Government. "Nebraska Facts." Retrieved August 1, 2009 (http://www.nebraska.gov/nebraskafacts.html).

Nebraska State Historical Society. "Blizzards." Retrieved August 23, 2009 (http://www.nebraskahistory.org/publish/publicat/timeline/blizzards.htm).

Nebraska State Historical Society. "Snowbound—The Blizzards of 1948–49." Retrieved August 23, 2009 (http://www.nebraskahistory.org/publish/publicat/timeline/snowbound_48-49.htm).

Nebraska Studies. "History Timeline." Retrieved August 1, 2009 (http://www.nebraskastudies.org).

Nebraska Studies. "Nebraska Hall of Fame." Retrieved October 5, 2009 (http://www.nebraskastudies.org/0000/fame.htm).

PBS. "New Perspectives on the West." Retrieved October 5, 2009 (http://www.pbs.org/weta/thewest).

Rolling Stone. "Bright Eyes." Retrieved October 5, 2009 (http://www.rollingstone.com/artists/brighteyes/biography).

Sartore, Joel. *Nebraska: Under a Big Red Sky.* Lincoln, NE: University of Nebraska Press, 2006.

Schmitt, Tom, ed. *Portraits of Nebraska.* Council Bluffs, IA: Nonpareil Publishing, 2004.

INDEX

About the Author

Jennifer Bringle has spent a lot of time in Nebraska through her job as a writer and editor and while visiting her aunt and cousins in McCook. She has also written several nonfiction books for teens and children.

Photo Credits

Cover (top left), p. 1 (left) © North Wind/Nancy Carter/North Wind Pictures; cover (top right), p. 1 (right) Nebraska/Collegiate Images/Getty Images; cover (bottom) Jodi Cobb/National Geographic/Getty Images; pp. 3, 6, 13, 14, 20, 25, 29, 38 © Shutterstock; p. 4 © GeoAtlas; p. 7 Michael S. Lewis/National Geographic/Getty Images; p. 9 Carl Iwasaki/Time-Life Pictures/Getty Images; p. 11 © www.istockphoto.com; p. 15 John C. H. Grabill/Getty Images; p. 18 © The Granger Collection; p. 19 © Nebraska State Historical Society neg. # RG1517:59-1; p. 21 © Nebraska.gov; p. 23 © www.istockphoto.com/Katherine Welles; pp. 24, 28 © AP Images; p. 26 Don Krump/The Image Bank/Getty Images; p. 30 © Chicago History Museum, USA/The Bridgeman Art Library; p. 31 © Warner Bros./Photofest; p. 33 New York Times Co./Getty Images; p. 35 Chris Machian/ Bloomberg via Getty Images; p. 39 (left) Courtesy of Robesus Inc.; p. 40 (left) © www.istockphoto.com/Nancy Nehring; p. 40 (right) © www.istockphoto.com.

Designer: Les Kanturek; Editor: Bethany Bryan;
Photo Researcher: Marty Levick